MY SONG IN THE NIGHT
Five American Folk-hymns

MACK WILBERG

MUSIC DEPARTMENT

OXFORD
UNIVERSITY PRESS

OXFORD
UNIVERSITY PRESS

198 Madison Avenue, New York, NY 10016, USA
Great Clarendon Street, Oxford OX2 6DP, England

Oxford University Press is a department of the University of Oxford.
It furthers the University's aim of excellence in research, scholarship,
and education by publishing worldwide

Oxford New York
Auckland Bangkok Buenos Aires Cape Town Chennai
Dar es Salaam Delhi Hong Kong Istanbul Karachi Kolkata
Kuala Lumpur Madrid Melbourne Mexico City Mumbai Nairobi
São Paulo Shanghai Taipei Tokyo Toronto

Oxford is a registered trademark of Oxford University Press

5 7 9 10 8 6 4

ISBN 978-0-19-380499-9

Music origination by Enigma Music Production Services, Amersham, Bucks, UK
Printed in the United States of America on acid-free paper

Contents

Orchestrations

Full scores and parts for an orchestral accompaniment are
available on rental from the publisher.

Amazing grace!

   3(picc).2.2.2 - 4.3.3.1 - timp - perc - bagpipes (opt.) - hp - org -str

Down to the River to Pray

   picc.2.2.2.2 - 4.3.3.1 - timp - 2 perc - banjo (opt.) - str

His voice as the sound

   3(picc).3.0.0.0 - rec (opt.) - 4.0.0.0 - hp - str

My God, My Portion, and My Love

   picc.2.2.2.2 - 4.3.3.1 - timp - 2perc - org - str

My Song in the Night

   3 hrns - hp - str

for the Mormon Tabernacle Choir and Orchestra at Temple Square

Amazing grace!

John Newton (1725–1807)

New Britain
The Southern Harmony
arr. **MACK WILBERG**
Organ by **David J. Hughes**

Sw: Tpt. 8' or Cornopean 8' Solo, Sw. to Ped
Gt: Foundations 8', Fl. 8', 4'
Ped: Foundations 16', 8'

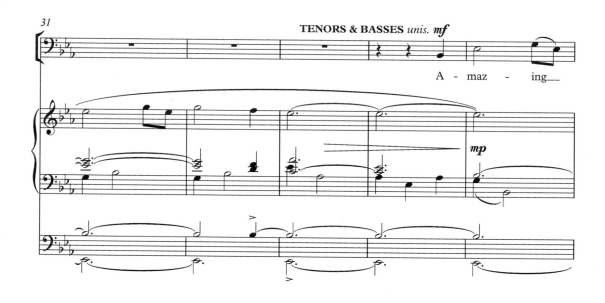

TENORS & BASSES *unis.* **mf**

A - maz - ing

mp

grace! how sweet the sound That saved a wretch like me!

Gt.

- Sw. to Ped.

shield and por- -tion__ be, As long as__ life en-

-dures.__

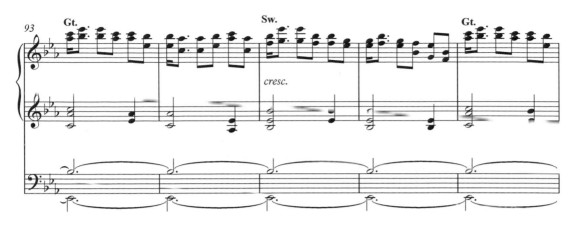

When we've been there ten thou - sand

When we've been there ten thou - sand

When we've been there ten thou - sand

When we've been there ten thou - sand

for the Timberline Middle School, Alpine, Utah,
Jennifer Halverson, Cathy Jolley, Kandis Taylor, conductors, Terry Hill, principal

Down to the River to Pray

Traditional American
arr. MACK WILBERG

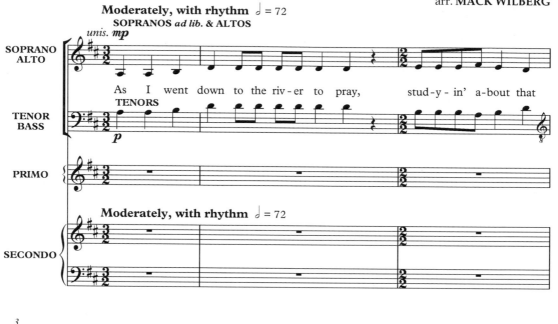

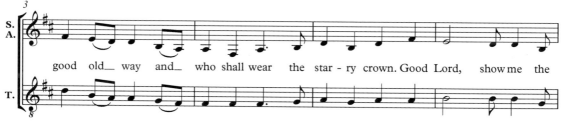

come on down, O, sis-ters, let's go down, down to the riv-er to

pray. O, sis-ters, let's go down, let's go down,

come on down, O, sis-ters, let's go down, down to the riv-er to

O, sis - ters, let's go down, down to the riv-er to pray.

O, fa-thers, let's go down, let's go down, come on down,

O mo-ther's let's go down, down to the riv-er to pray.

18

SOPRANOS & ALTOS *unis.* **f**

As I went

TENORS & BASSES *unis.*

down to the riv-er to pray, stud-y-in' a-bout that good old__ way and

who shall wear the robe and crown. Good Lord, show me the way!

for the Mormon Tabernacle Choir and the Orchestra at Temple Square

His voice as the sound

Samanthra
The Southern Harmony
WILLIAM WALKER
arr. Mack Wilberg

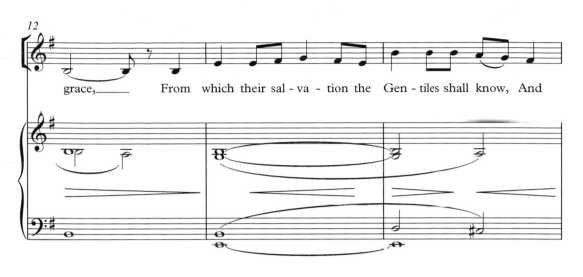

grace,_____ From which their sal - va - tion the Gen - tiles shall know, And

bask in the smile of His face.

30

47

div. TUTTI *unis.*

mp

(oo) He___ looks and ten thou-sands of an - gels re-joice, And

mp

(oo) He___ looks, and ten thou-sands of an - gels re-joice, And

(oo)_____

mp

50

S.
A. *unis.*

myr - i-ads wait for His word,_____ He speaks and e - ter - ni - ty

T.
B.

(oo)_____

for the Armstrong Atlantic State University Chorale, Savannah, Georgia, David Brown, director.

My God, My Portion, and My Love

Isaac Watts (1674–1748)

Dunlap's Creek
The Southern Harmony
F. LEWIS
arr. Mack Wilberg

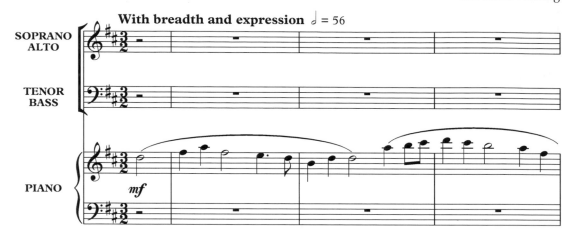

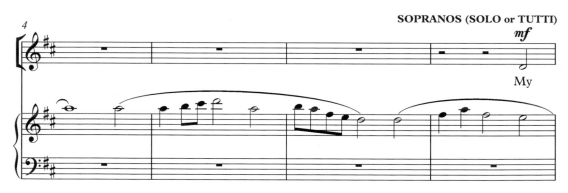

that sits up - on the throne, And to a-dore the

Him that sits up - on the throne, And to a-dore the

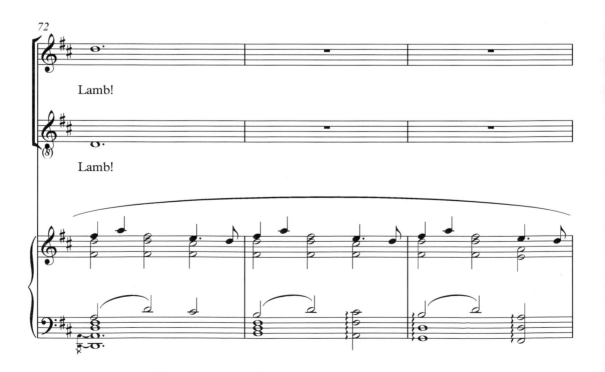

Lamb!

Lamb!

Of Him that sits up - on_ the_ throne, And

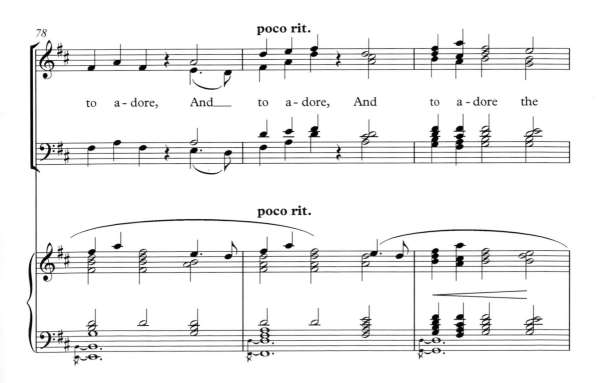

to a - dore, And_ to a - dore, And to a - dore the

42

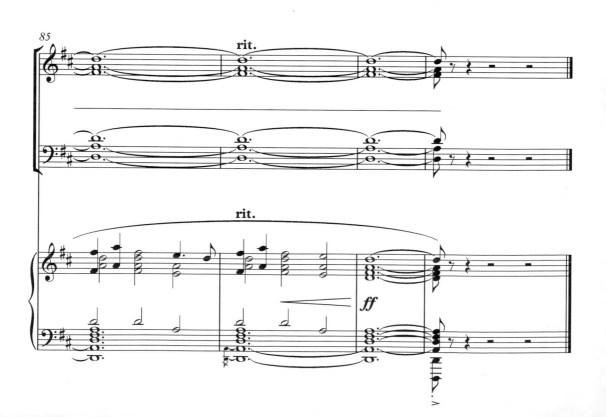

Presented to Dr. Paul Magyar by the Adult Choir of Tallowood Baptist Church,
Houston, Texas, in honor of his tenth anniversary as Minister of Music

My Song in the Night

Expression
American Folk-hymn
arr. **MACK WILBERG**

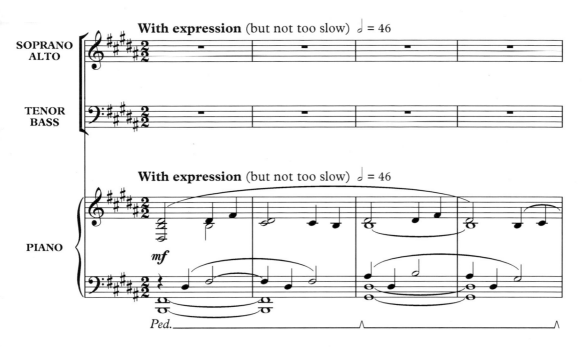

Je - sus, my Sav - ior, my song in the night, Come to

(Ped.)

us with Thy ten - der love, my soul's__ de - light, Un - to

(Ped.)

Thee_____ O__ Lord in af - flic - tion I

(Ped.) _____ sim.

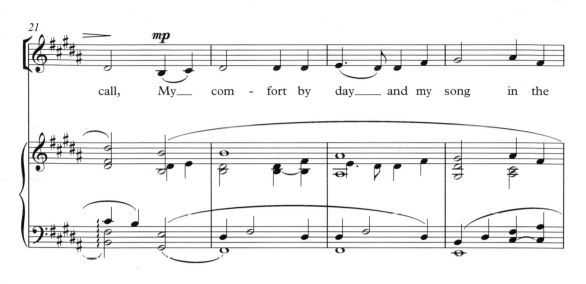

call, My__ com - fort by day__ and my song in the

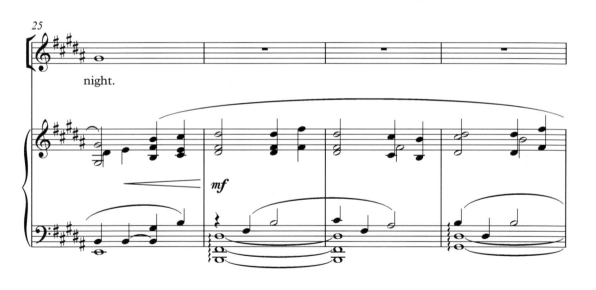

night.

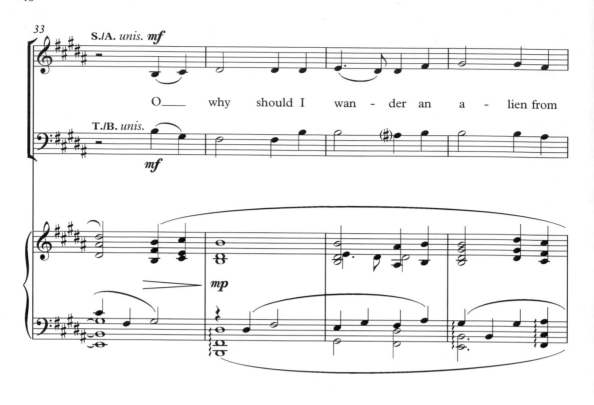

O__ why should I wan - der an a - lien from

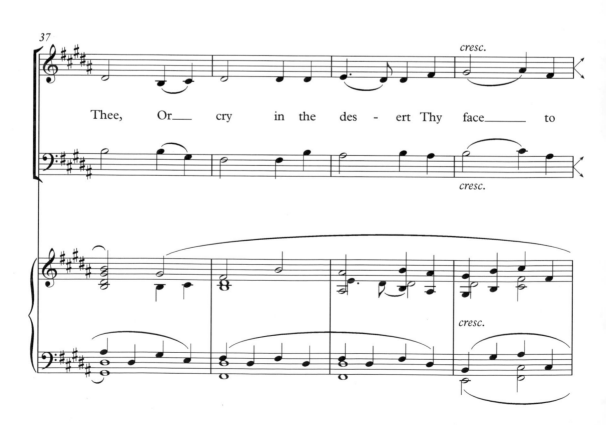

Thee, Or__ cry in the des - ert Thy face____ to

song   in   the   night.

song   in   the   night.____

song   in   the   night.

song   in   the   night.

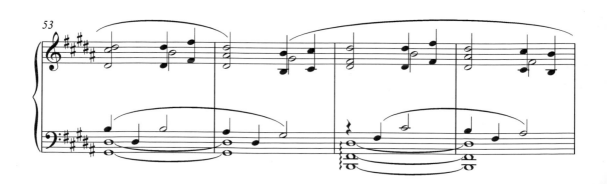

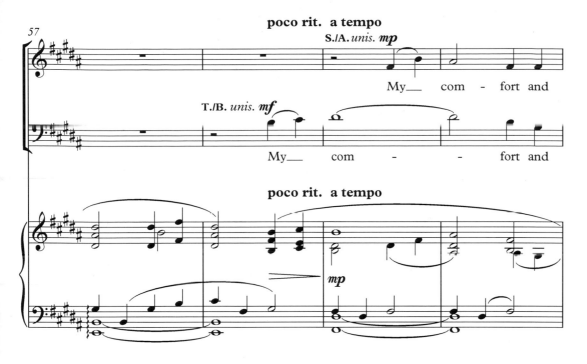

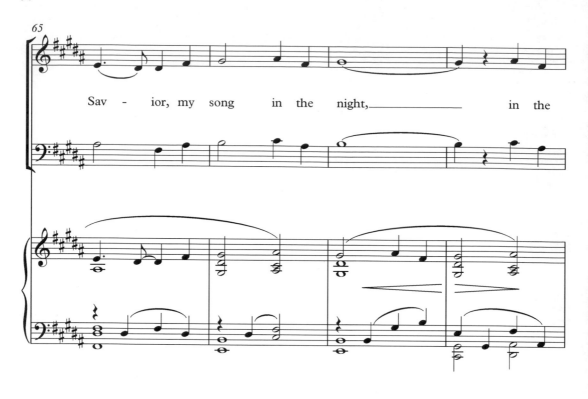

Sav - ior, my song in the night,_____ in the

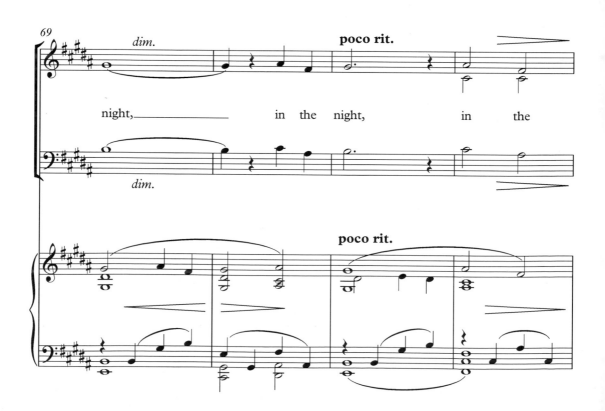

night,_____ in the night, in the

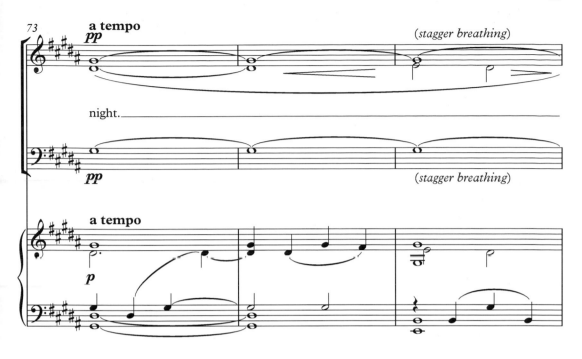

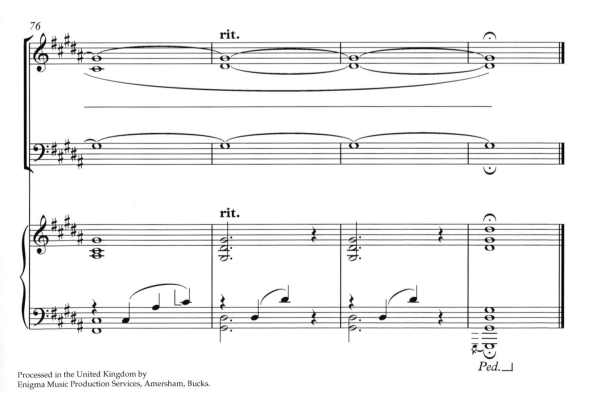

Processed in the United Kingdom by
Enigma Music Production Services, Amersham, Bucks.